SHARDS

OF

TIME

SAINT JULIAN PRESS

POETRY

Praise for **Shards of Time**

This fine new poetry of Maryam Hiradfar takes the reader toward a vision of both cosmos and human experience: the meeting of a supernal world and affective quotidien life. This is vision at its best, founded upon the variety of emotion as it exists in time, for the book takes the reader on a journey of moral and spiritual transition where metaphors startle and vivify us with profoundly gorgeous clarity. This poetry captures and expresses small unbreakable shards of human truth with sonority, kindness, and glimpses of absolute beauty.

—Kevin McGrath
Department of South Asian Studies
Harvard University

"I have been water and iron," writes Maryam Hiradfar, and in these visionary poems, she indeed proves that her soul contains multitudes, fruitful contradictions, different mysteries. By turns feral, steady, sorrowing, joyous, Apollonian, Dionysian, these poems are a refreshing voice in the world of contemporary poetry. "I wonder what it means to breathe," she muses. And these poems show us.

—Joseph Fasano
The Last Song of the World

During her second book of poetry, *Shards of Time*, Maryam Hiradfar walks the reader through the world we both live in and imagine with a most insightful and gentle voice. Expressing soulfully her wonder for ourselves ~ her gorgeous poems enter our minds with "...words twirling." Allow yourself a moment with *Shards,* and your heart and soul will be given "... the beat of our endless pondering."

—Dr. Gary Geissler
Poetic in the Gray

The meaning of Time follows us every day of our lives. In this profound series of poems, Maryam Hiradfar evokes our disparate ways of experiencing Time: a flowing river, an ebbing tide, a chilling wind, a piercing arrow, a beat of the heart, a breath. Time is a fleeting moment, the jagged bits of a shattered mirror. And yet, even in a jagged fragmented shard, we can see a shimmering wholeness. These poems are a gift to us in our journey in Time.

—Diana Eck
Professor of Religion
Harvard University

SHARDS

OF

TIME

MARYAM HIRADFAR

SAINT JULIAN PRESS
HOUSTON

Published by
SAINT JULIAN PRESS, Inc.
2053 Cortlandt, Suite 200
Houston, Texas 77008

www.saintjulianpress.com

ISBN-13: 978-1-955194-20-4
Library of Congress Control Number: 2023944697

Cover Art Credit: Maryam Hiradfar

To Maman & Baba

CONTENTS

PREFACE

I've often pondered a question that may sound deceptively simple: How can we live in the present without getting stuck there? It's a thought that's been the driving force behind *Shards of Time*. As I penned each piece, I found myself silently responding:

The secret lies in recognizing that moments are like a river, ever-flowing. Stagnation occurs when we dwell on the past or fixate on the future, neglecting the unfolding and fluid "now."

Through *Shards of Time*, I invite you to join me on a journey through the intricate fragments of our existence. Amid these fragments, you'll discover ambition and doubt, triumphs, and despair. I invite you to feel and think about how time is continuous and granular and how each moment is unique.

In these words, I hope you'll find a reflection of your own experience and meditate on each fragment as a vital part of a larger fluid journey. It's about acknowledging life's continuity while honoring each moment's unique character.

Time's passage may blur these fragments, but within their distinctiveness lies the story of us. So, may this collection serve as a mirror for reflection and a vessel for your soul's journey.

Warmly,
Maryam

"You are the universe in ecstatic motion."

-Rumi

S HA R DS

O F

T I M E

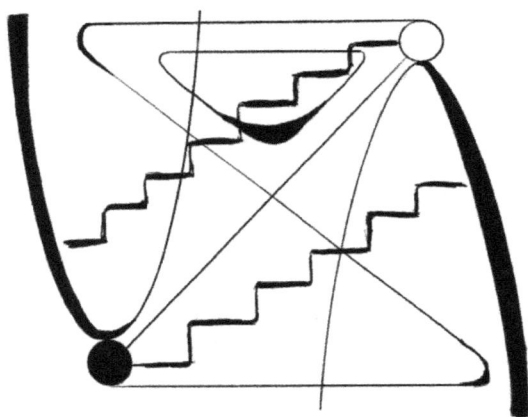

TORRENTS AT DAWN

Entanglements

Time has its cunning ways
of twisting and turning your senses
burning what seems to be water
and making iron flow like a river

I have been both
I have been water and iron
I have burned and I have flowed
yet today, I am neither

Today, I sit at the perfect intersection
of doubt and of hope
of rising and of falling
of death and of rebirth

Yet, just as nature demands
that we reach for the surface
when we are short of breath
my eyes reach for the light
of that most distant star

Today, I dare myself to prove
that improbable dreams combined
don't become less probable
but that they beat in resonance
that they multiply

Today, I dare you
that most distant star
to do the same
sing with me, beat with me

And while I am as still as a stone
if reality grants its hand
I will be powder
I will be smoke
forever, and forevermore.

Dawn is loved forever

Day is offering
lighthearted as a dove
and plain as the blanket
of morning mist
Dawn is loved forever

Quenching our thirst
as we revolve
in the never-ending cycles
and moments that engulf us
in their ever-stretching fabric
pinned between the two ends
of the revolving horizon
Dawn is loved forever

Yet the passage
of this beloved orb
against the infinite landscape
decorated with time
prefers now over all history
and gently puts to rest
all hopes of a juxtaposed dance
of now and infinity
Dawn is loved forever

And in its embracing warmth
moments are eclipsed
washed out like sand
the stars wish
for daytime darkness
to momentarily reveal
their long-held secrets
when the shadow
of a cold stone falls
on all that ever longs for light
and the world dives into silence
in awe
Dawn is loved forever.

Fragments of a Breath

A breath so alive
turns into reminiscence
then a memory
later a flashback

Down the road a marking
a time stamp
and in the end, history
worn out, and misty

After the edges of papers
have turned yellow
yellow corners curled up
cover covered with dust
sheets wrinkled like our skin
skin turned into dust
when the ink is dissolved
and so is our blood
when the soft flesh is gone
crows' sunset feast adjourned
when we are dispersed
through the river currents
on the wings of the wind
on yellow pollens a bee carries
in the body of a flower vase
in the warm blood
of an albatross flying free
in the deep blue of a heron's wings
in the azure of eyes born anew
in the breath of a singing Robin

A breath is still alive
Multiplied
Sung
Relived
Reborn
Reimagined
Without us
for us, it does not need
the self-sufficient force
running free & feral.

A Moral Dilemma

Is it time to mourn the death of a dream
or to celebrate the death of an illusion?

Comedy of appetite
preferring the taste
of our habits to novelty
our longing to our arrival
and lamenting over our losses
to celebrating a clean window-glass

Try your try human
but in the end
can you remove the taboo
of your spirit
smiling at death?

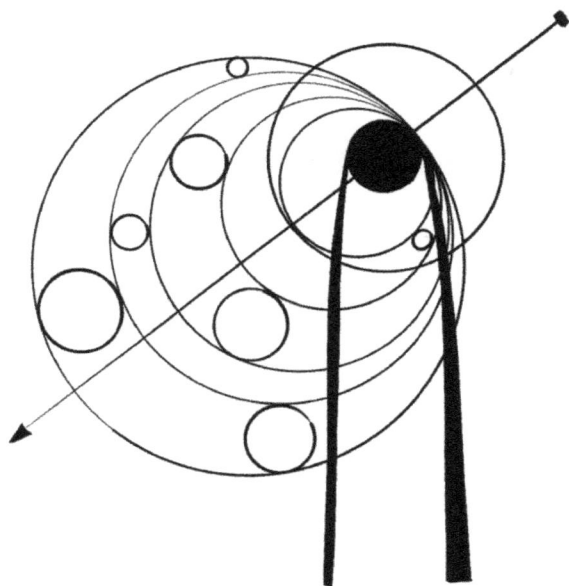

PARALYSIS

Shards

The moment has no mercy
for beauty nor for elegance
perfection transforms
into a distorted image

Shards pierce
the flesh of reason
and the mind bleeds.

Dreams are mirrors
when shattered you are left
with a thousand fragments
to sweep off the floors

Yet among the pain
if you stand still for a moment
the thousand pieces
stare back at you

Each holding now
the image of a new whole.

The Flame

Bring your hands close
surround the thin body
of the candle whose eyes
sting the wind of time

Let yourself surround
yourself and be assured
that a breeze brightens
the flame of a burning desire.

Corkscrew

On the face of the paper
two dimensions
easy to envision
a circle, the cross section
of a reality in three dimensions
of the corkscrew
you walk on, in one direction
Say goodbye forever
to your beginning step
you thought you walked a full circle
you will never meet it again
but you will turn and turn
certain that you will reach it again
lost on your sheet
of the promising circle.

Lunulata

Light as a leaf
stretched as a new canvas
her body rests on the water
that has made an offer
to bear it all

The weight
and the compression
the dust and the old scars
all that there ever was

What remains is a clear frame
for unfinished brushstrokes
and half-written words
buoyant and asleep it floats
bridging the dark ocean rocks
and the exploding hearts
of ancient stars.

The Silent Saxaul Tree

From time to time
you will see
the silent Saxaul tree
with its roots embraced
by the ochre clay sand
by the barren land
bearing not even
a pearl of water

From time to time
you will see
the silent Saxaul
its leaves motionless
its body still as a steel pillar
you will dream of the dance
of the swaying poplars
by the singing river

The silent Saxaul too
dreams of laughter with the wind
yet, its whispers may crack
the fragile shell of the land
while in its tears
a wild beige rose might grow
in silver silence.

The Wall

The door is closed
the curtain's drawn
particles glow
in the beam of light
that creeps into the lonely room

Our lonely room
the lonely room that has no tongue
to speak its loneliness
our lonely room that has no eyes
to cry its emptiness
our lonely room that stands
brick by brick
by the force of the mortar
that wants to scream
from the pain of the weight
of our heaviness
our bitterness
our simultaneous loneliness

The door is closed
the wall watches itself
in the hollow eternity of the mirror
it watches its pale white body
the pale white body that encloses our bodies
from time to time
it watches and watches and gasps
at its fantastic incapability
to enclose our souls

It watches and watches and gasps
at the fantastic hypocrisy of its role
to enclose and not enclose at the same time

To be a mask of togetherness
to be the weakest and sturdiest frame
to be the interior reflection of our exteriors

Only our exteriors
the exteriors that we choose
for the sake of the wall
for the sake of the pale white wall
for it has to enclose something
and that something can only
of course, can only be our exteriors

Why you might ask?
first close the door
the white wall shall not hear
what I'm about to say

Now we are safe
So you asked why?
because we fear
that God forbid
a human eye might see through
the red watery eyes of another

Because we fear
that God forbid,
we will panic at the sight
of such Eternity
that surpasses any wall
any lock
any chain

Because we fear
that God forbid
Eternity would engulf us
because we fear
my friend
we fear the Eternity
the power
the love
of our interiors.

We fear the Infinity of our smooth
calm Human interiors,
we fear the Infinity of our Human souls
that can't be
can't possibly be enclosed

So we stare
and the throatless tongueless white wall
screams its heart out
and the mirror echoes the quiet shriek
in the hollow shell of the room

My friend,
now that we have heard the wall's plea
let us do it a favor
tonight
when the moon comes out
we'll take a brush and a bucket of paint
pitch black, we'll cover every inch of its body
and we'll take it down
kindly
brick by brick

Then
we'll sit under the moonlight
with our eternal interiors watching
the infinite borderless Universe that would not fit
in that room that is no longer there

For we are
and we now can admit for the first time
Humans.

And the tired bricks
rest in peace.

Arrow of Time

I wonder what it means
to breathe
when every heartbeat
is the ticking of a clock
when every breath
is a stretching of a bow
to thrust a timid arrow
at a flying dove

Every heartbeat is a second
and I am stuck
in a cycle of time quickening
under my pacing heart
my heartbeat quickening
under the racing time

Would it freeze the arrow
would it crack the bow
would the dove stay still
if the beating stopped?
motionless, I know
that time can stop the beat
but the beat can't stop the flow
of the quickening time.

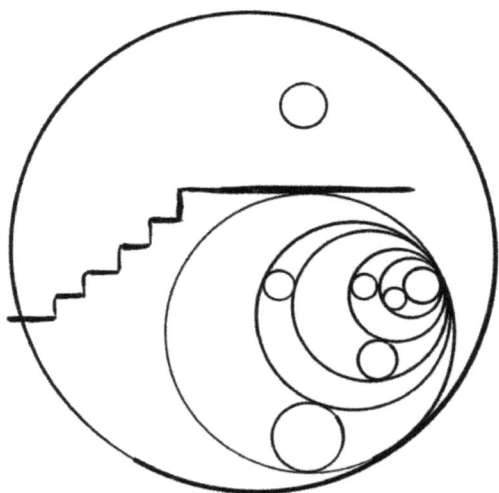

BUOYANCY

Gallery of Thoughts

Among the stretches of space
there is room for anything
for rings of smoke
for a valley
for Sorrow
even for the young Desire
you have convinced yourself
no infinity can keep

There's a gallery of thoughts
floating on the moon
where nothing ever stirs
and no wind ever blows
where thoughts just hang
and unfurl
for you to walk among and observe.

NEOWISE

What binds us is a voyage
you set ablaze by the sun
we set adrift toward your light
both searching for the Sublime

Roads asleep under the rhyme
of whispering crickets, their lullaby
the only sound heard in the void
besides the pounding heart of time

Restless searching through the dark
every faint star sings of hope
like a lighthouse, far their flicker
guiding us to a distant shore

Traveling light-years with a turn
of a few degrees of sight
we are pilgrims of the Cosmos
sailing upward towards the light

Just as eyes are turning down
and as our hearts are turning dark
a firefly of green and gold hue
takes our glances toward the spark

Felicity is a still moment
pinned on the evening vault
a pearl on the velvet blue sky
bringing Time to an utter halt

Motionless, silent and young
life is kneeling bare and meek
eyes are drinking wine of Wonder
drunk as Coexistence speaks.

Violet Night

They rose with the moon
by the drowning sun
light minds and memories
bound by images floating

Their bodies, branches shivering
embracing their flaming hearts
beating to the pulse of the river
forever flowing toward the stars

Fragments, they thought of
confessions of a faraway mind
time knows no dimensions
now fragments burn and shimmer

Tides caress their footsteps
every evening and dawn
reverberations of their laughter
persist under the sleepy bridges

The moon had confessed long ago
before the river and the sunken sun
that no embrace was ever warmer
than their glances merging into one.

Red Tailed Hawk

Perching high up on the oak branch
shaking free with winds winter
ruby eyes of warm, inciting
primal pride of life unhindered

Flight of shadows seeking shelter
under faint unthreatening starlight
a moment's pause descending to enter
dreams of sleepers through the night

Light and fast a breath in hurry
melts snowflakes to dreams and dust
with waking the flight departed
clarity's gone and memories lost.

The Fourteenth

It is the fourteenth
moon hunter's evening
horizon is bathed in lilac
clouds and silk blue skies
lingering a thought may crack
at any breath and rise
up to the darkened heart
of a blackhole.

To never be found again
to never rise or fall
but to hang still
and to defeat the infinity
of the slowing time.

Buoyancy

These days gravity fades
lightly as a breath on the mirror
beneath it buoyancy sleeps
calmly with no anticipation

What moved once no longer does
rising smoke and falling rain
nor does pain penetrate
or love fall.

Motion's hunger to fade
the once unnoticeable edges
is silent today, today sharp resolution
punctures every psyche into attention

This is a moment to hold
the wings of the hummingbird
this is when the train never leaves
when midnight never arrives

This is breath at its finest balance
between rising inhalation
and a falling sigh.

The Heart of The Charles

The heart of the river, it beats
as it did in the nights long ago
when the moon was shining above
when silence had not yet grown

The heart of the river, it beats
to the same old melody of rotations
around the sun and around the galaxies
through the timeless mirror of our reflections

The heart of the river, it beats
still, even though moments have passed
even though footprints have faded now
and the Heron has flown over the broken glass

The heart of the river, it beats
to the beat of our endless pondering
for it has been given a heart of peace
for it has survived through doubt and wandering

The heart of the river, it beats
it will keep on performing its symphony
beyond the evening when ours will
no longer beat with it in harmony
.
.
.

so listen now, beat now, beat now
beat until it lasts...

The Quiet Corner

Come to the quiet corner
where meaning lies bare at rest
come to the center of disguise
to the kingdom of essence, undressed

Come to the pinnacle of Glory
arching low beneath the ocean
where words are muted and silent
in tune with waves of demotion

What casts us in gold and amber
what reaches for breath, eternal
was drunken youth, unwitting
gazing at the chilling wind of time

Though weightlessness and tragedy
hand in hand float in this ocean
ours is moment's gift of movement
low, quiet, and steady in motion.

The Eternal Companion

Walking down below the shadows
looking far across the mind
voice of doubt kneeled and whispered:
"say it clearly, say it loud"

Take the shadow of the pine tree
cast it on my sleeping heart
rest your head upon my shoulder
let the silence beg the start

We have torn the mist of daybreak
we have tied the hands of night
from the depth of every cavern
we have summoned ghosts of light

Chasing moths with midnight candles
watching clouds from dusk to dawn
time has found its way of resting
now behind all curtains drawn

Lightning burnt the leaves of maple
standing proud, upon the hill
sweet is life without a burden
bare and dancing in the wind

Take the oar and row forever
there's a shore behind the clouds

No one knows who's reached the ending
ocean breeze sweeps out the doubts.

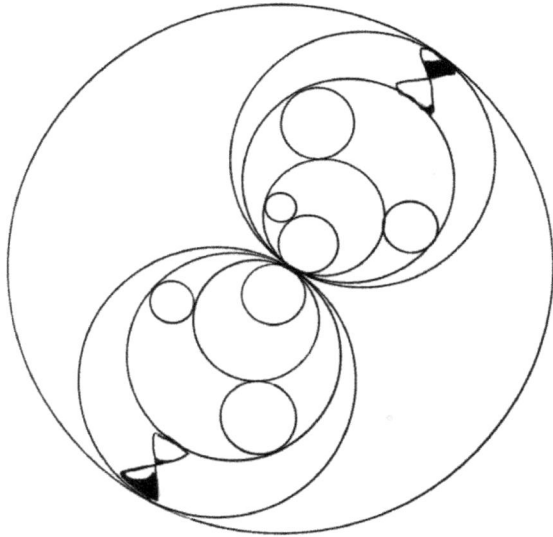

ARRIVAL

Arrival of the Albatross

It approaches from a distance
a point of moving blue
gradually gaining size
like a dead body finding soul

Its massive body displaces
the air, your attention
and everything that can ever stir
larger than life, larger than thought

Cruising on the molten steel
waves of silver and gold
carry the shadow of this infinite bird
to encircle you in its warmth

The moment has arrived
when moments move no more
except for those that count
the heartbeats of the albatross

No waves, wind, or breeze
a quiet space with ease
has been arranged for you to hear
the whispers of the bird of dreams.

The Pilgrim

Streams may flow
ice may grow
but when let free
a stone gently
sinks to the bedrock
where Peace is still
where Peace is sane
where Peace belongs
where Peace came from

"All seek the Origin"
all return to Tranquility
through torrents at dawn.

Infinite Dunes

In the presence of light
it is only light we can sing of
in its absence
its luminous memory

In the fleeting warmth of a candlelight
there's only a few tales to read
in the hushed light
thousands untold to whisper

In every grain of sand that falls
only a few glances to exchange
in the broken hourglass
dunes of them to long for

We are bound, momentarily
as grains
blowing on the wind

as tales exchanged
as glances merged

in time
we shimmer
till the hourglass breaks
.

.

And forever now
we are infinite dunes.

Smoke Signal

A thought is a cloud
of smoke emerging
within the air dispersing
in a single breath
no trace, no tint, no scent
remaining
where was the flame?

A thought is a cloud
words twirling
in moments repeating
mind, hushing every spark
gasping
a frozen river begs: "I'm cold
where is the flame?"

A thought is a cloud
words convincing
like gold written
in an angel's letters
you must be a fool asking
where is the flame?

A thought is a cloud
madness dancing, in awe
the world stands, the breeze
holds its breath, the smoke
hanging still, clear, glittering
"where is the flame?"

Rotations Around Dawn

Standing on the edge of water
clarity offers itself, shimmering
as stars melt in waves of silver

A soft rotation into the light
unfolds the moments to be
as we roll toward the horizon

Cartography of time
is spread upon the sky
for you to read, to explore

No one ever needs to try
at dawn, there are no secrets
only familiar faces of mind

To try at this fragile moment
is to break the china of light
into blue fragments of the usual

Trust the brushstrokes of the wind
to dissolve dreams of the night
into wakefulness of dawn

I relinquish my weight to gravity
and let the palms of the breeze
decide the fate of today's dive.

Pelicans Appear

Persistent is the sound
"I pass, but I will reappear
lookup, see me fly above"
the warmness for a moment
leaves no space for fear

Absent-mindedly I turn
"yes I do"
I see the pelicans above
synchronous with the thought
the flying train out of the smoky blue

Synchronous with the childlike voice
synchronous with the strummed chords
dreams have shattered
into the souls of pelicans
as the wind of wonder blows

No wonder they look ancient
they carry the flames of hushed candles
a fire no longer on paraffin
burning blinks in the eyes of the pelicans
the trapped soul of the terrapin

I bask in the longing
that in the field of their bird's eye view
I am as clear as a fish
reaching the surface of the water, blue
enough to be taken by their caravan
to the land of hidden treasures.

Coyotes

Their sound
invisible
as masked as the image of a gnome
that hides behind
the bushes and wildflowers
at the corner of the backyard
where the abandoned cabin
has been sleeping

They howl in a cacophony
as jokingly
as the carnival of the dead
as grievously
as the screaming siren
of an ambulance
they accompany the melodies
of the highway

Time after time
performing their howling ritual
responding to the conscience
of their soft midnight soul
they are the sound of cycles
of dusk and dawn
of birth and death
never neglecting

They make appearance
in my midday conversations
uninterrupted
and leave their shadow
as their echo dies down
and gives way
to the humming noise
of the passing cars

Friends of dawn
primal simplicity of thought
the unpredictable familiar instinct
I can rest assured
that they will return
once the highway calls them again.

ACKNOWLEDGMENTS

I would like to express my deepest gratitude to Prof. Kevin McGrath, the esteemed Poet in Residence at Lowell House. Your unwavering mentorship and support have been the guiding light on my poetic path. You have not only helped me and my poetic voice but also nurtured it, and for that, I am immensely grateful.

I extend my heartfelt thanks to the Lowell House Poemical Society and all its members. Your camaraderie and the shared passion for poetry have been a constant source of inspiration. Your recitations and willingness to listen to my words have touched my heart and enriched my creative journey.

To my parents, whose love for poetry sparked my own from a young age, I owe a debt of gratitude. Thank you for introducing me to the timeless works of classical and modern Persian poets. Your guidance and encouragement have shaped my appreciation for the beauty of words.

Writing this book would not have been possible without the support and inspiration of these incredible individuals and communities. I am deeply fortunate to have you all as a part of my poetic world.

With sincere appreciation,
Maryam

ABOUT THE AUTHOR

Maryam Hiradfar is an emerging writer whose roots can be traced back to the literary landscapes of classical Persian literature. Her work brings a distinct blend of cultures and experiences to her artistic expressions. Growing up encircled by the rhythmic verses of classic Persian poets like Rumi and Hafez, plus modern luminaries such as Sohrab Sepehri and Ahmad Shamlou, Maryam became infused with the essence of Persian poetry from an early age.

Maryam's childhood was a tapestry of memories spent memorizing the enchanting poetry of Hafez – a cherished tradition shared among the young. Venturing across continents, Maryam's path led her to Harvard College, where she pursued a study of physics. Guided by a fascination with the world's intricate beauty, Maryam's verses weave together the wonders of the physical realm with the intricacies of human emotions.

Amidst her academic pursuits, Maryam found a nurturing haven within the Lowell House Poemical Society, where her passion for poetry flourished. This creative sanctuary became the birthplace of her original works and a space to refine her unique voice. Her poetry, which bears the visual imprints of her love for illustration and photography, offers a fusion of imagery and language that resonates deeply.

Roadside, Maryam's first poetry collection, marked a milestone in her artistic journey. She invites readers into her world through her verses and camera lens, offering an intimate glimpse of her perspective. Maryam embarks on a new chapter with her latest creation, *Shards of Time*. This collection marries minimalistic graphics with poetic narratives, crafting a mosaic of feelings and moments that transcend the boundaries of traditional expression.

Typefaces Used

TYPEFACE GARAMOND - Garamond
PERPETUA TITLTING MT – LIGHT

www.ingramcontent.com/pod-product-compliance
Lightning Source LLC
Chambersburg PA
CBHW020217090426
42734CB00008B/1107